HOW TO KNOW THE FOUR TEMPERAMENTS

"Unlocking Your True Self and Mastering Interpersonal Dynamics"

VINCENT HOWELL

Copyright ©

Dedication

Dedicated to those on the quest for self-awareness and harmony in relationships, may this book serve as a guiding light in understanding the intricacies of human temperament. Here's to embracing diversity, fostering empathy, and forging connections that enrich our lives and communities.

Table of Contents

Acknowledgments

I extend my heartfelt gratitude to all who contributed to the creation of this book. Special thanks to the readers, my mentors, family, and friends, for their unwavering support, encouragement, and invaluable insights throughout this journey. Your dedication has truly enriched the pages of this work and made it possible.

Preface

In this preface, I extend my warmest welcome to you, the reader, as we embark together on a transformative journey of self-discovery and interpersonal understanding. "How to Know the Four Temperaments" is a testament to the enduring fascination with human behavior and the timeless quest to unravel the mysteries of the human psyche.

In the following pages, we delve into the rich tapestry of temperament theory, tracing its origins and evolution through history. We explore the intricate interplay of the four primary temperaments—Choleric, Melancholic, Sanguine, and Phlegmatic—and delve into the unique characteristics, strengths, and challenges of each.

This book is not merely an intellectual exploration; it is a practical guide for navigating the complexities of human interaction with empathy and wisdom. Whether you seek to deepen your understanding of yourself, enhance your relationships, or cultivate leadership skills, the insights offered here will serve as a beacon of light on your path.

As we journey together through these pages, I invite you to approach this exploration with an open mind and a willingness to embrace the diversity of human experience. May this book empower you to unlock your true potential, foster deeper connections with others, and embark on a journey of personal growth and fulfillment?

Thank you for joining me on this adventure.

Chapter 1:

Introduction to Temperament Theory

- Understanding the Historical Roots

Temperament theory has deep roots in ancient philosophy and medicine, with origins dating back to the times of Hippocrates, the Greek physician often referred to as the father of medicine. Hippocrates proposed that human behavior and personality were influenced by the balance of bodily fluids, or "humors," namely blood, phlegm, yellow bile, and black bile.

Building upon Hippocrates' foundations, subsequent scholars and philosophers such as Galen expanded and refined the theory of temperaments. Galen classified temperaments into four primary types, corresponding to the four senses of humor: choleric, melancholic, sanguine, and phlegmatic. These temperaments were believed to influence not only personality traits but also physical health and predispositions to illness.

Temperament theory continued to evolve throughout the Middle Ages and Renaissance, influencing fields as diverse as psychology, medicine, and literature. However, it wasn't until the modern era that temperament theory experienced a resurgence of interest, particularly with the work of psychologists such as Carl Jung and William Marston.

Today, while contemporary psychology has moved away from the strict physiological basis of temperament theory, the core concepts continue to inform our understanding of personality and behavior. By exploring the historical roots of temperament theory, we gain valuable insights into the enduring fascination with understanding what makes us tick and how we interact with the world around us.

- Overview of the Four Temperaments

The four temperaments—choleric, melancholic, sanguine, and phlegmatic—have been central to understanding human behavior and personality for centuries. Each temperament is characterized by distinct patterns of thought, emotion, and behavior, providing valuable insights into how individuals interact with the world and with each other.

1. Choleric: Individuals with a choleric temperament are often described as assertive, ambitious, and goal-oriented. They tend to be decisive leaders who thrive in positions of authority and responsibility. Cholerics are driven by a

desire for control and achievement, and they excel in situations that require strategic planning and problem-solving.

2. Melancholic: Melancholic individuals are introspective, sensitive, and empathetic. They possess a deep emotional depth and are often drawn to artistic and creative pursuits. Melancholics tend to be perfectionists who strive for excellence in everything they do, but they may also struggle with feelings of self-doubt and insecurity.

3. Sanguine: Sanguine individuals are outgoing, enthusiastic, and sociable. They have a natural charm and charisma that draws others to them, and they thrive in social situations. Sanguines are spontaneous and adventurous, often seeking out new experiences and opportunities for excitement and pleasure.

4. Phlegmatic: Phlegmatic individuals are calm, easygoing, and even-tempered. They are known for their patience, tolerance, and ability to remain composed under pressure. Phlegmatics are skilled mediators and peacekeepers who value harmony and stability in their relationships and environments.

While each temperament has its unique strengths and weaknesses, no one temperament is inherently better or worse than the others. Instead, understanding the four temperaments allows us to appreciate the diversity of human nature and to recognize the value that each individual brings to our lives and communities.

- Importance of Temperament in Personal and Professional Life

Temperament plays a crucial role in shaping our personal and professional lives, influencing everything from our relationships and career choices to our communication styles and leadership abilities. Understanding our temperament and the temperaments of those around us can have profound implications for our success, happiness, and overall well-being.

1. Self-awareness: Recognizing our temperament allows us to better understand our strengths, weaknesses, and tendencies. By understanding our natural inclinations and preferences, we can make more informed decisions about

our goals, aspirations, and areas for personal growth.

2. Relationship dynamics: Temperament influences how we interact with others and how we perceive their behavior. By understanding the temperaments of our friends, family members, and colleagues, we can navigate relationships more effectively, communicate more empathetically, and resolve conflicts more constructively.

3. Career satisfaction: Our temperament can shape our career interests, work styles, and job preferences. For example, a choleric individual may thrive in a high-pressure, leadership role, while a melancholic individual may excel in a creative or analytical profession. By aligning our career choices with our temperament, we can find greater

fulfillment and success in our professional lives.

4. Leadership effectiveness: Effective leadership requires an understanding of both one's temperament and the temperaments of those we lead. A Skilled leader can adapt their communication style, decision-making approach, and motivational strategies to accommodate the diverse temperaments of their team members, fostering collaboration, innovation, and productivity.

5. Conflict resolution: Temperament-aware individuals are better equipped to navigate conflicts and disagreements in both personal and professional settings. By recognizing the underlying temperamental differences that contribute to conflict, we can approach resolution with empathy,

patience, and a willingness to compromise.

In essence, the importance of temperament in personal and professional life lies in its ability to enhance self-awareness, improve relationship dynamics, guide career choices, enhance leadership effectiveness, and facilitate conflict resolution. By embracing the diversity of temperaments and leveraging their unique strengths, we can cultivate more fulfilling and harmonious lives, both personally and professionally.

Chapter 2:

The Choleric Temperament

- Characteristics and Traits of Choleric Individuals

Choleric individuals are characterized by their assertiveness, ambition, and strong leadership qualities. They possess a natural drive and determination to achieve their goals, often displaying high levels of confidence and decisiveness in their actions. Here are some key characteristics and traits commonly associated with the choleric temperament:

1. Assertiveness: Cholerics are known for their assertive nature and their willingness to take charge in various situations. They are not afraid to speak their minds or assert their opinions, often taking on leadership roles and guiding others toward a common goal.

2. Ambition: Cholerics are highly ambitious individuals who are driven by a desire for success and achievement. They set high standards for themselves and are willing to work hard and overcome obstacles to reach their goals.

3. Competitiveness: Cholerics thrive in competitive environments and are often drawn to challenges that allow them to demonstrate their skills and abilities. They enjoy pushing themselves to excel and strive to outperform others in their pursuits.

4. Decisiveness: Cholerics are decisive decision-makers who can quickly assess situations and take action. They are not afraid to make tough choices and are often seen as confident and decisive leaders.

5. Independence: Cholerics value their independence and autonomy, preferring to take control of their destinies rather than relying on others. They are self-reliant individuals who are not afraid to take risks and pursue their goals independently.

6. Directness: Cholerics are known for their direct communication style and their ability to get straight to the point. They value efficiency and effectiveness in their interactions and may come across as blunt or straightforward in their communication.

7. Impatience: Cholerics have a low tolerance for inefficiency and may become frustrated or impatient when faced with obstacles or delays. They prefer to work at a fast pace and may become frustrated with those who do not share their sense of urgency.

8. Short Temper: In moments of stress or frustration, choleric may display a short temper or become irritable and impatient with others. They may struggle to maintain their composure when faced with challenges or setbacks.

Overall, choleric individuals possess a unique combination of assertiveness, ambition, decisiveness, and independence that sets them apart in both personal and professional settings. While they may face challenges such as impatience and a short temper, their strong leadership qualities and determination make them valuable assets in any endeavor.

- Strengths and Weaknesses of the Choleric Temperament

Choleric individuals possess a variety of strengths that contribute to their success and effectiveness in various areas of life. However, like any temperament, they also face certain weaknesses that can present challenges in personal and professional relationships. Here are some key strengths and weaknesses of the choleric temperament:

Strengths:

1. Leadership Skills: Cholerics are natural-born leaders who excel in positions of authority and responsibility. They possess strong leadership qualities such as assertiveness, decisiveness, and strategic thinking, making them effective at guiding and motivating others toward a common goal.

2. Ambition and Drive: Cholerics are highly ambitious individuals who are driven by a desire for success and achievement. They set high goals for themselves and are willing to work hard and overcome obstacles to reach them.

3. Problem-Solving Abilities: Cholerics are adept at analyzing complex situations and coming up with practical solutions. They have a strong ability to think critically and creatively, allowing them to

overcome challenges and find innovative ways to achieve their objectives.

4. Confidence and Assertiveness: Cholerics exude confidence and assertiveness in their actions and decisions. They are not afraid to speak their minds or assert their opinions, which can inspire confidence and respect in others.

5. Independence and Self-Reliance: Cholerics value their independence and autonomy and are comfortable taking initiative and making decisions on their own. They are self-reliant individuals who do not need constant guidance or validation from others.

Weaknesses:

1. Impatience: Cholerics have a low tolerance for inefficiency and may

become frustrated or impatient when faced with obstacles or delays. Their sense of urgency can sometimes lead to impulsive decision-making or a lack of consideration for others' perspectives.

2. Short Temper: In moments of stress or frustration, choleric may display a short temper or become irritable and impatient with others. They may struggle to maintain their composure and may be prone to outbursts of anger or frustration.

3. Insensitive Communication: Cholerics are known for their direct communication style, which can sometimes come across as blunt or insensitive. They may unintentionally offend others with their straightforwardness and may struggle to consider the feelings or sensitivities of those around them.

4. Dominance and Control Issues: Cholerics may tend to dominate or control others, especially in group settings or professional environments. Their assertiveness and desire for control can sometimes lead to conflicts or power struggles with colleagues or subordinates.

5. Difficulty Delegating: Cholerics may have difficulty delegating tasks or trusting others to take on responsibilities. They may prefer to take on a heavy workload themselves rather than risk relying on others who may not meet their high standards or expectations.

Overall, while the choleric temperament offers many strengths in terms of leadership, ambition, and problem-solving abilities, it also presents challenges such as impatience, a short temper, and difficulties with communication and interpersonal relationships. Recognizing and addressing these weaknesses can help cholerics cultivate more effective and harmonious interactions with others.

- **Strategies for Harnessing Choleric Energy**

Choleric individuals possess a wealth of energy and drive that, when harnessed effectively, can lead to great success and achievement. By understanding their temperament and implementing strategies to channel their energy constructively, choleric can maximize their potential and thrive in various aspects of life. Here are some strategies for harnessing choleric energy:

1. Set Clear Goals: Cholerics thrive on having clear goals and objectives to work towards. By setting specific, measurable, and achievable goals, they can focus their energy and efforts on tasks that align with their ambitions and priorities.

2. Prioritize Tasks: Cholerics often tend to take on too much at once, leading to overwhelm and burnout. To avoid spreading themselves too thin, they should prioritize tasks based on their importance and urgency, focusing on high-impact activities that align with their long-term goals.

3. Develop Time Management Skills: Cholerics can benefit from honing their time management skills to maximize productivity and efficiency. By creating

schedules, setting deadlines, and breaking tasks down into manageable chunks, they can ensure that they make the most of their time and avoid procrastination.

4. Delegate Responsibility: Cholerics may have difficulty delegating tasks to others, fearing that they won't meet their high standards or expectations. However, learning to delegate effectively can free up time and energy for more strategic activities, allowing them to focus on their core strengths and priorities.

5. Practice Emotional Regulation: Cholerics may struggle with impulsivity and anger management, especially in high-pressure situations. Learning to recognize and regulate their emotions can help them maintain composure and make rational decisions, even in challenging circumstances.

6. Seek Feedback and Collaboration: Cholerics can benefit from seeking feedback and collaboration from others, especially those with different perspectives and expertise. By actively listening to others' ideas and opinions, they can gain valuable insights and perspectives that can inform their decision-making and problem-solving processes.

7. Maintain Work-Life Balance: Cholerics may tend to prioritize work over other areas of life, leading to imbalance and burnout. They need to make time for rest, relaxation, and leisure activities to recharge their batteries and maintain overall well-being.

8. Cultivate Empathy and Understanding: Cholerics can enhance their interpersonal skills by cultivating

empathy and understanding towards others. By taking the time to consider others' perspectives and feelings, they can build stronger relationships and foster a more collaborative and supportive work environment.

By implementing these strategies, choleric can harness their energy and drive in a way that leads to greater success, fulfillment, and well-being in both their personal and professional lives.

Chapter 3:

The Melancholic Temperament

- Identifying Melancholic Tendencies and Behaviors

The melancholic temperament is characterized by introspection, sensitivity, and a deep emotional depth. Individuals with a melancholic temperament often exhibit certain tendencies and behaviors that distinguish them from other temperaments. Here are some key characteristics to help identify melancholic tendencies:

1.   Introspection: Melancholics   are introspective by nature, often spending a significant amount of time reflecting on their   thoughts,   emotions,   and experiences. They have a rich inner world and may be drawn to solitary activities such as reading, writing, or artistic pursuits.

2. Sensitivity: Melancholics are highly sensitive individuals who are deeply attuned to their own emotions and the emotions of others. They may be more prone   to   mood   swings   and   may experience emotions such as sadness, anxiety, or empathy more intensely than others.

3. Perfectionism: Melancholics have a tendency towards perfectionism and may set high standards for themselves and others. They strive for excellence in

everything they do and may become frustrated or disappointed when they fall short of their expectations.

4. Pessimism: Melancholics may tend towards pessimism or negative thinking, often focusing on the potential pitfalls or drawbacks of a situation rather than the positives. They may be more prone to worry or anxiety, especially in uncertain or stressful situations.

5. Reserved Demeanor: Melancholics often have a reserved or quiet demeanor, preferring to observe and listen rather than actively participate in social interactions. They may be more comfortable expressing themselves through written or artistic mediums rather than verbal communication.

6. Attention to Detail: Melancholics are detail-oriented individuals who have a

keen eye for nuance and subtlety. They may excel in tasks that require careful attention to detail, such as editing, research, or artistic craftsmanship.

7. Empathy and Compassion: Despite their struggles, melancholics are often highly empathetic and compassionate towards others. They have a deep understanding of human emotions and may be drawn to helping professions or advocacy work.

8. Difficulty Letting Go: Melancholics may have difficulty letting go of past hurts or regrets and may ruminate on negative experiences long after they have occurred. They may also hold grudges or dwell on perceived slights, making forgiveness and moving on challenging.

By recognizing these tendencies and behaviors, individuals with a melancholic temperament can gain a better understanding of themselves and how they interact with the world around them. Embracing their unique strengths and challenges can lead to greater self-awareness, personal growth, and fulfillment.

- Coping with Melancholic Challenges

Individuals with a melancholic temperament may encounter specific challenges related to their sensitive and introspective nature. However, various coping strategies can help them navigate these challenges and maintain their well-being. Here are some effective coping mechanisms:

1.   Self-Compassion: Practicing self-compassion involves treating oneself with kindness and understanding, especially during difficult times. Melancholics can benefit from cultivating self-compassion by acknowledging their struggles without judgment and offering themselves the same level of care and support they would offer to others.

2.   Mindfulness and Meditation: Mindfulness techniques and meditation practices can help melancholics ground themselves in the present moment and cultivate a greater sense of calm and clarity. By focusing on their breath or observing their thoughts without judgment, they can reduce anxiety and rumination and enhance their overall well-being.

3. Expressive Arts Therapy: Engaging in creative outlets such as writing, painting, or music can provide a powerful means of self-expression and emotional release for melancholics. Expressive arts therapy allows them to channel their innermost thoughts and feelings into a tangible form, promoting healing and self-discovery.

4. Seeking Support: Melancholics may benefit from seeking support from friends, family members, or mental health professionals. Sharing their feelings and experiences with trusted individuals can provide validation, empathy, and practical advice for coping with challenges.

5. Setting Boundaries: Establishing clear boundaries with others can help melancholics protect their emotional well-being and prevent burnout. By

communicating their needs and limits assertively, they can ensure that they have the time and space they need for self-care and rejuvenation.

6. Practicing Gratitude: Cultivating a daily gratitude practice can help melancholics shift their focus from negative thoughts to positive aspects of their lives. Taking time to reflect on the things they are grateful for can promote a sense of perspective and resilience in the face of adversity.

7. Physical Self-Care: Engaging in regular exercise, maintaining a healthy diet, and prioritizing adequate sleep are essential aspects of self-care for melancholics. Physical activity releases endorphins, improves mood, and reduces stress, while proper nutrition and rest support overall well-being and resilience.

8. Professional Help: In some cases, melancholics may benefit from professional help such as therapy or counseling. A trained therapist can provide guidance, support, and evidence-based interventions to help them manage symptoms of depression, anxiety, or other mental health challenges.

By implementing these coping strategies, individuals with a melancholic temperament can cultivate resilience, enhance their well-being, and navigate life's challenges with greater ease and grace.

- Cultivating Balance and Resilience for Melancholic Types

While melancholic individuals may face unique challenges due to their sensitive and introspective nature, there are several strategies they can employ to cultivate balance and resilience in their lives. By incorporating these practices into their daily routine, melancholics can enhance their well-being and cope more effectively with life's ups and downs. Here are some ways to cultivate balance and resilience:

1. Self-Care Rituals: Establishing regular self-care rituals can help melancholic

individuals prioritize their mental, emotional, and physical well-being. This may include activities such as meditation, journaling, taking long baths, or spending time in nature—anything that helps them relax and recharge.

2. Mindfulness Practices: Practicing mindfulness involves bringing awareness to the present moment without judgment. Melancholics can benefit from mindfulness techniques such as deep breathing exercises, body scans, or mindful walking to help them stay grounded and centered amidst the turmoil of their emotions.

3. Healthy Boundaries: Setting healthy boundaries with others is crucial for protecting their energy and emotional well-being. Melancholics should learn to recognize their limits and assertively communicate their needs to others,

whether it's taking time alone to recharge or saying no to additional commitments when they're feeling overwhelmed.

4. Creative Expression: Engaging in creative pursuits such as writing, painting, or playing music can provide an outlet for melancholic individuals to express themselves and process their emotions. Creative expression allows them to channel their innermost thoughts and feelings into something tangible, fostering a sense of catharsis and self-discovery.

5. Social Support: Building a strong support network of friends, family members, or like-minded individuals can provide invaluable emotional support and validation for melancholic individuals. Having someone to confide in during difficult times can help them

feel less isolated and more resilient in the face of adversity.

6. Positive Relationships: Cultivating positive and nurturing relationships with others is essential for melancholic individuals to thrive. Surrounding themselves with people who accept and appreciate them for who they are can boost their self-esteem and sense of belonging, contributing to their overall well-being.

7. Flexibility and Adaptability: Practicing flexibility and adaptability in their thinking and behavior can help melancholic individuals navigate life's inevitable changes and challenges with greater ease. Being open to new experiences and perspectives allows them to grow and evolve, fostering resilience in the face of adversity.

8. Seeking Professional Help: In some cases, melancholic individuals may benefit from seeking professional help such as therapy or counseling. A trained therapist can provide additional support, guidance, and coping strategies to help them manage their emotions and navigate life's challenges more effectively.

By incorporating these practices into their lives, melancholic individuals can cultivate greater balance, resilience, and well-being, allowing them to embrace their sensitive nature and thrive in all aspects of life.

Chapter 4:

The Sanguine Temperament

- Exploring the Energetic and Sociable Nature of Sanguine Individuals

The sanguine temperament is characterized by its energetic and sociable nature, making sanguine individuals natural extroverts who thrive in social settings. They possess a zest for life and a magnetic personality that draws others to them. Here's a deeper exploration of the energetic and sociable nature of sanguine individuals:

1.	Outgoing Personality: Sanguine individuals are known for their outgoing and vivacious personality. They are often the life of the party, exuding enthusiasm and energy wherever they go. Their friendly and approachable demeanor makes it easy for them to strike up conversations and make new friends.

2. Optimism and Positivity: Sanguines have an inherently optimistic outlook on life and tend to see the glass as half full rather than half empty. They approach challenges with a can-do attitude and a belief that things will work out for the best, which can be contagious and uplifting to those around them.

3.	Adaptability and Spontaneity: Sanguines are highly adaptable individuals who thrive on spontaneity and excitement. They are always up for trying new things and embracing new experiences, whether it's traveling to a new destination, trying a new hobby, or attending a spontaneous event.

4. Charisma and Charm: Sanguines possess a natural charm and charisma that makes them incredibly likable and charismatic. They have a knack for making others feel special and valued, and they excel in social situations where they can shine and captivate an audience.

5. Storytelling and Humor: Sanguines are often gifted storytellers and entertainers who can hold a crowd's attention with their lively anecdotes and infectious laughter. They have a quick wit and a playful sense of humor that adds joy and levity to any gathering.

6. Empathy and Emotional Intelligence: Despite their outgoing nature, sanguines are also empathetic individuals who are

attuned to the emotions of others. They have a natural ability to connect with people on an emotional level and provide comfort and support when needed.

7. Networking and Relationship Building: Sanguines excel in networking and relationship building, forging connections with people from all walks of life. They thrive in social environments where they can meet new people, exchange ideas, and foster meaningful relationships.

8. Enthusiasm for Life: At the core of the sanguine temperament is an unbridled enthusiasm for life and all its possibilities. Sanguines approach each day with a sense of excitement and anticipation, eager to make the most of every moment and embrace the adventures that lie ahead.

Overall, the energetic and sociable nature of sanguine individuals makes them invaluable assets in social and professional settings. Their charisma, optimism, and ability to connect with others contribute to their success and fulfillment in all aspects of life. Empathy and Emotional Intelligence: Despite their outgoing nature, sanguines are also empathetic individuals who are attuned to the emotions of others. They have a natural ability to connect with people on an emotional level and provide comfort and support when needed.

- Navigating Sanguine Strengths and Pitfalls

Sanguine individuals possess a range of strengths that contribute to their vibrant and outgoing nature, but they also face certain pitfalls that can impact their well-being and relationships. Navigating these strengths and pitfalls effectively can help sanguine individuals harness their energy and maximize their potential. Here's how to navigate the strengths and pitfalls of the sanguine temperament:

Strengths:

1. Charisma and Charm: Sanguines have a natural charisma and charm that makes them highly likable and influential in social situations. They can use their charm to build rapport, inspire others, and create positive connections.

2. Optimism and Enthusiasm: Sanguines possess an innate optimism and enthusiasm for life that is contagious to those around them. They can use their positive outlook to motivate others, uplift spirits, and foster a sense of hope and possibility.

3. Adaptability and Flexibility: Sanguines are adaptable individuals who thrive in dynamic and unpredictable environments. They can use their flexibility to navigate change, overcome obstacles, and seize new opportunities with ease.

4.   Networking and Relationship Building: Sanguines excel in networking and relationship building, forging connections with people from all walks of life. They can use their social skills to expand their social circle, cultivate valuable contacts, and advance their personal and professional goals.

Pitfalls:

1. Impulsivity and Lack of Focus: Sanguines may struggle with impulsivity and a tendency to jump from one idea or activity to another without fully considering the consequences. They can mitigate this pitfall by practicing mindfulness, setting priorities, and cultivating discipline in their decision-making.

2. Overcommitment and Burnout: Sanguines may tend to overcommit

themselves due to their enthusiastic nature and desire to please others. They can avoid burnout by learning to set boundaries, prioritize self-care, and delegate tasks when necessary.

3. Attention-Seeking Behavior: Sanguines may seek validation and attention from others to bolster their self-esteem and confidence. They can overcome this pitfall by cultivating a sense of self-worth independent of external validation, focusing on their strengths and accomplishments.

4. Difficulty with Follow-Through: Sanguines may struggle with follow-through and consistency in their pursuits, as they may lose interest or enthusiasm once the initial excitement wears off. They can address this pitfall by setting realistic goals, breaking tasks into

smaller steps, and holding themselves accountable for their actions.

By navigating these strengths and pitfalls with awareness and intention, sanguine individuals can cultivate a healthy balance in their lives and relationships. They can leverage their charisma, optimism, and adaptability to thrive in various endeavors while mitigating the challenges that may arise along the way.

- Maximizing Productivity and Well-being as a Sanguine Personality

As a sanguine personality, you possess a natural zest for life and boundless energy that can propel you to achieve great things. By leveraging your strengths and implementing strategies to manage potential pitfalls, you can maximize your productivity and well-being. Here are some tips to help you thrive:

1. Set Clear Goals: Channel your enthusiasm and energy into setting clear, achievable goals for yourself. Break down larger goals into smaller, actionable steps to maintain focus and momentum.

2. Prioritize Tasks: Identify your most important tasks and prioritize them

based on their impact and urgency. Focus on completing high-priority tasks first to ensure progress toward your goals.

3. Use Time Management Techniques: Harness your adaptability to experiment with different time management techniques and find what works best for you. Consider using techniques such as the Pomodoro Technique or time-blocking to structure your day and maximize productivity.

4. Limit Distractions: Sanguines may be easily distracted by new ideas or opportunities. Create a conducive work environment by minimizing distractions such as social media, email alerts, or unnecessary noise.

5. Practice Mindfulness: Cultivate mindfulness practices such as meditation or deep breathing exercises to ground

yourself in the present moment and maintain focus amidst distractions. Mindfulness can help you manage stress and enhance overall well-being.

6. Set Boundaries: Sanguines may tend to overcommit themselves, leading to burnout. Learn to set boundaries and say no to additional commitments when necessary to protect your time and energy.

7. Delegate Tasks: Recognize that you can't do everything on your own. Delegate tasks that are not essential for you to handle personally, allowing you to focus on your strengths and priorities.

8. Take Breaks: Allow yourself regular breaks throughout the day to recharge and prevent burnout. Use breaks to engage in activities that rejuvenate you,

such as taking a short walk, listening to music, or practicing a hobby.

9. Celebrate Progress: Acknowledge and celebrate your accomplishments along the way, no matter how small. Celebrating progress can boost motivation and reinforce positive habits.

10. Practice Gratitude: Cultivate gratitude by reflecting on the things you're grateful for each day. Gratitude can help shift your focus from what's lacking to what's abundant in your life, fostering a sense of fulfillment and well-being.

By implementing these strategies, you can harness your sanguine personality traits to maximize productivity and well-being in both your personal and professional life. Embrace your enthusiasm and optimism while staying mindful of potential pitfalls, and you'll be well-equipped to achieve success and fulfillment.

Chapter 5:

The Phlegmatic Temperament

- Understanding the Calm and Easygoing Nature of Phlegmatic Types

The phlegmatic temperament is characterized by its calm, easygoing, and even-tempered nature. Individuals with a phlegmatic temperament tend to approach life with a sense of tranquility and inner peace, preferring harmony and stability over conflict and drama. Here's a deeper exploration of the calm and easygoing nature of phlegmatic types:

1. Tranquility and Serenity: Phlegmatic individuals exude a sense of tranquility and serenity in their demeanor and interactions with others. They have a calming presence that can help diffuse tension and create a peaceful atmosphere in any situation.

2. Emotional Stability: Phlegmatics are known for their emotional stability and resilience in the face of adversity. They have a steady temperament and are less likely to be swayed by external circumstances or fluctuations in mood.

3. Patience and Tolerance: Phlegmatics possess a high degree of patience and tolerance, allowing them to remain composed and understanding even in challenging or frustrating situations. They are adept at handling conflict with grace and diplomacy, preferring to seek

compromise and resolution rather than escalate tensions.

4. Empathy and Compassion: Despite their calm exterior, phlegmatic individuals are deeply empathetic and compassionate towards others. They have a genuine concern for the well-being of those around them and are often sought out as trusted confidants and advisors.

5. Practicality and Realism: Phlegmatics are grounded in reality and tend to approach life with a practical and pragmatic mindset. They are not easily swayed by fanciful ideas or unrealistic expectations, preferring to focus on what is feasible and achievable.

6. Consistency and Reliability: Phlegmatics are known for their consistency and reliability in their

actions and commitments. They are dependable individuals who follow through on their promises and can be counted on to fulfill their obligations.

7. Adaptability and Flexibility: While phlegmatics may prefer stability and routine, they are also adaptable and flexible when necessary. They can adjust to changes and transitions with ease, remaining calm and composed in the face of uncertainty.

8. Conflict Avoidance: Phlegmatics tend to avoid conflict and confrontation whenever possible, preferring to maintain harmony and peace in their relationships and environments. They may shy away from expressing their own needs or opinions to avoid rocking the boat.

Overall, the calm and easygoing nature of phlegmatic individuals contributes to their ability to navigate life's challenges with grace and resilience. Their emotional stability, empathy, and practicality make them valuable assets in personal and professional relationships, fostering a sense of harmony and cooperation wherever they go.

- Embracing Phlegmatic Strengths in Relationships and Work

Phlegmatic individuals bring a unique set of strengths to their relationships and work environments, fostering harmony, stability, and cooperation. By embracing these strengths, phlegmatics can enhance their interpersonal dynamics and excel in their professional endeavors. Here's how to embrace phlegmatic strengths in relationships and work:

1. Calm Communication: Utilize your calm and even-tempered nature to foster open and respectful communication in relationships and work settings. Your ability to remain composed and level-headed, even in challenging situations, can diffuse tension and promote understanding among others.

2. Active Listening: Embrace your empathy and compassion by practicing active listening in conversations. Take the time to fully understand the perspectives and feelings of others before offering your input or solutions. Your attentive listening can make others feel valued and understood.

3. Conflict Resolution: Lean into your preference for harmony and stability when navigating conflicts in relationships or work dynamics. Approach disagreements with a focus on finding common ground and compromise rather than escalating tensions. Your diplomatic approach can help facilitate peaceful resolutions.

4. Reliability and Dependability: Embrace your consistency and reliability in your work commitments and relationships. Follow through on your promises and obligations consistently, demonstrating to others that they can trust and rely on you to deliver results.

5. Adaptability and Flexibility: Utilize your adaptability and flexibility to navigate changes and challenges in both personal and professional settings.

Embrace new opportunities and approaches with an open mind, demonstrating your willingness to adjust and evolve as needed.

6. Problem-Solving Skills: Embrace your practical and pragmatic mindset to approach problems and challenges with a solutions-oriented mindset. Use your logical thinking and analytical skills to identify practical solutions and overcome obstacles effectively.

7. Supportive Presence: Embrace your supportive presence in relationships and work environments by offering a steady and reassuring presence to those around you. Your calm demeanor and empathetic nature can provide comfort and stability to others during times of stress or uncertainty.

8. Collaboration and Teamwork: Embrace your cooperative spirit by actively participating in collaborative efforts and team projects. Your willingness to work harmoniously with others and contribute to collective goals can foster a sense of camaraderie and synergy within teams.

By embracing these strengths, phlegmatic individuals can cultivate fulfilling and productive relationships and excel in their professional pursuits. Their calm, empathetic, and reliable nature makes them valuable assets in any context, fostering a sense of harmony and cooperation wherever they go.

-Strategies for Motivating and Engaging Phlegmatic Individuals

Motivating and engaging phlegmatic individuals may require a different approach compared to other temperaments, as they tend to value stability, harmony, and calmness. Here are some strategies to effectively motivate and engage phlegmatic individuals:

1. Provide Clear Expectations: Phlegmatic individuals thrive in environments where expectations are clearly communicated and defined. Provide them with clear goals, objectives,

and timelines to give them a sense of structure and direction.

2. Offer Recognition and Appreciation: Acknowledge and appreciate the contributions of phlegmatic individuals regularly. Offer praise and recognition for their consistent reliability, dependability, and steady performance.

3. Foster a Supportive Environment: Create a supportive and nurturing work environment where phlegmatic individuals feel valued and respected. Encourage open communication, collaboration, and mutual support among team members.

4. Encourage Autonomy: Allow phlegmatic individuals the autonomy to work independently and at their own pace. Avoid micromanaging and trust

them to manage their responsibilities effectively.

5. Provide Opportunities for Growth: Offer opportunities for phlegmatic individuals to develop their skills, expand their knowledge, and take on new challenges. Provide training, mentorship, and career development opportunities to help them grow professionally.

6. Tap into Their Interests: Identify the interests and passions of phlegmatic individuals and align tasks and projects with their areas of interest whenever possible. Engaging them in work that resonates with their interests can increase their motivation and enthusiasm.

7. Break Tasks into Manageable Steps: Break down larger tasks into smaller, more manageable steps to prevent

overwhelm and facilitate progress. Phlegmatic individuals may appreciate having a clear roadmap to follow and achieve their goals gradually.

8. Encourage Work-Life Balance: Promote work-life balance and well-being initiatives to support the overall health and happiness of phlegmatic individuals. Encourage them to take breaks, recharge, and prioritize self-care to maintain their energy and motivation.

9. Provide Constructive Feedback: Offer constructive feedback to phlegmatic individuals in a supportive and encouraging manner. Focus on highlighting their strengths and areas for improvement, and offer guidance on how they can continue to grow and develop.

10. Celebrate Achievements: Celebrate milestones and achievements with phlegmatic individuals to acknowledge their progress and contributions. Create a positive and celebratory atmosphere that reinforces their sense of accomplishment and motivation.

By implementing these strategies, you can effectively motivate and engage phlegmatic individuals, tapping into their strengths and creating an environment where they can thrive and contribute their best work.

Chapter 6:

Integrating the Four Temperaments

- Recognizing the Interplay of Temperaments in Society and Culture

Understanding the interplay of the four temperaments—sanguine, choleric, melancholic, and phlegmatic—in society and culture provides valuable insights into human behavior, relationships, and societal dynamics. By recognizing and integrating the diverse perspectives and strengths of each temperament, we can foster greater harmony, cooperation, and understanding in our communities. Here's how the four temperaments intersect and interact in society and culture:

1.	Diverse Perspectives: Each temperament brings a unique set of strengths, preferences, and tendencies to the table. By recognizing and appreciating the diverse perspectives of individuals with different temperaments, we can leverage their strengths and contributions to enrich our collective understanding and decision-making processes.

2. Complementary Roles: The four temperaments often complement each other in various roles and contexts. For example, sanguine individuals may excel in social settings and relationship-building, while choleric individuals may thrive in leadership and

decision-making roles. By recognizing and valuing the contributions of individuals with different temperaments, we can create more balanced and effective teams and organizations.

3. Conflict Resolution: Understanding the temperamental differences between individuals can facilitate more effective conflict resolution and communication strategies. By recognizing that conflicts may arise due to differences in temperament rather than personal attacks, we can approach disagreements with greater empathy, understanding, and respect for diverse perspectives.

4. Cultural Dynamics: The interplay of temperaments also influences cultural dynamics and societal norms. For example, cultures that value assertiveness and ambition may exhibit a higher prevalence of choleric traits, while

cultures that prioritize harmony and collectivism may align more closely with phlegmatic tendencies. By recognizing and understanding these cultural dynamics, we can navigate cross-cultural interactions with greater sensitivity and awareness.

5. Personal Development: Understanding our own temperament and the temperaments of others can enhance personal development and interpersonal relationships. By recognizing our strengths, weaknesses, and preferences, we can tailor our communication and behavior to better connect with others and navigate social dynamics effectively.

6. Social Change and Progress: Integrating the four temperaments can also inform efforts for social change and progress. By recognizing the diverse perspectives and contributions of

individuals with different temperaments, we can foster more inclusive and equitable societies that value the unique strengths and experiences of all members.

Overall, integrating the four temperaments in society and culture requires a nuanced understanding of human behavior, relationships, and societal dynamics. By recognizing and valuing the diverse perspectives and contributions of individuals with different temperaments, we can create more harmonious, inclusive, and resilient communities that embrace the richness of human diversity.

- Creating Harmonious Relationships and Teams Across Temperament Types

Building harmonious relationships and teams across different temperament types requires understanding, empathy, and effective communication. By leveraging the strengths of each temperament and fostering a culture of respect and collaboration, individuals can work together synergistically to achieve shared goals. Here's how to create harmonious relationships and teams across temperament types:

1. Recognize and Appreciate Differences: Acknowledge and appreciate the diverse strengths, preferences, and

communication styles of individuals with different temperaments. Recognize that each temperament brings unique perspectives and contributions to the table, and value the richness of this diversity.

2. Build Trust and Respect: Foster a culture of trust and respect where individuals feel valued and respected for who they are. Encourage open communication, active listening, and empathy to create an environment where everyone feels heard and understood.

3. Encourage Collaboration: Emphasize the importance of collaboration and teamwork in achieving shared goals. Encourage individuals to work together across temperament types, leveraging each other's strengths and expertise to achieve greater success collectively.

4. Communicate Effectively: Tailor communication strategies to accommodate the diverse communication styles of individuals with different temperaments. Be clear, concise, and direct in your communication, while also being sensitive to the needs and preferences of others.

5. Balance Leadership Styles: Recognize that effective leadership may look different depending on the temperament of the leader and team members. Balance assertiveness with empathy, and adapt your leadership style to accommodate the needs and preferences of individuals with different temperaments.

6. Manage Conflict Constructively: Address conflicts and disagreements promptly and constructively, focusing on finding mutually beneficial solutions.

Encourage individuals to express their concerns openly and respectfully, and facilitate productive dialogue to resolve conflicts amicably.

7. Celebrate Diversity: Celebrate the diversity of temperament types within your relationships and teams, recognizing that each individual brings unique strengths and perspectives to the table. Foster a culture of inclusion and appreciation for the richness of human diversity.

8. Promote Self-Awareness and Growth: Encourage individuals to cultivate self-awareness and personal growth by reflecting on their own temperament traits and how they impact their interactions with others. Provide opportunities for individuals to develop their emotional intelligence and interpersonal skills.

9. Lead by Example: Model inclusive and collaborative behavior as a leader or team member, demonstrating respect, empathy, and effective communication in your interactions with others. Lead by example and inspire others to follow suit in building harmonious relationships and teams.

By implementing these strategies, individuals and teams can create harmonious relationships and work together effectively across temperament types. Embrace the diversity of temperaments, leverage each other's strengths, and foster a culture of respect, collaboration, and mutual support to achieve shared success.

- Personal Growth and Development Through Temperament Awareness

Temperament awareness can be a powerful tool for personal growth and development, helping individuals better understand themselves, navigate relationships, and maximize their potential. By gaining insight into their own temperament traits and those of others, individuals can cultivate self-awareness, empathy, and resilience. Here's how temperament awareness can contribute to personal growth and development:

1. Self-Understanding: Temperament awareness allows individuals to gain insight into their own unique strengths, weaknesses, preferences, and tendencies.

By understanding their temperament traits, individuals can identify areas for growth, capitalize on their strengths, and make informed decisions aligned with their values and goals.

2. Emotional Intelligence: Recognizing how temperament influences emotions, behavior, and interpersonal dynamics can enhance emotional intelligence. Individuals can learn to regulate their emotions, empathize with others, and communicate effectively, leading to more fulfilling relationships and greater overall well-being.

3. Relationship Building: Temperament awareness facilitates more harmonious and effective relationships by helping individuals understand and appreciate the differences in temperament among their family members, friends, and colleagues. By recognizing and respecting

the diverse perspectives and communication styles of others, individuals can build stronger, more resilient relationships based on trust, respect, and mutual understanding.

4. Conflict Resolution: Understanding how temperament influences conflict styles and preferences can improve conflict resolution skills. Individuals can learn to navigate conflicts constructively, de-escalate tensions, and find mutually acceptable solutions by adapting their communication and conflict resolution strategies to accommodate the temperament of those involved.

5. Personal Effectiveness: Temperament awareness enables individuals to leverage their strengths and manage their weaknesses more effectively. By aligning their goals, tasks, and activities with their temperament traits, individuals can

enhance their productivity, motivation, and satisfaction in various aspects of their personal and professional lives.

6.   Leadership   Development: Temperament awareness is essential for effective leadership development. Leaders who understand their own temperament and the temperaments of their team members can tailor their leadership styles, communication strategies, and motivational techniques to accommodate the diverse needs and preferences of their team, fostering a culture of trust, collaboration, and high performance.

7.   Resilience   and   Adaptability: Temperament awareness promotes resilience and adaptability in the face of challenges and setbacks. By recognizing their own coping mechanisms and stress responses, individuals can develop

healthy coping strategies, build resilience, and thrive in times of change and adversity.

8. Continuous Learning and Growth: Temperament awareness is an ongoing journey of self-discovery and growth. Individuals can continue to deepen their understanding of temperament and its impact on their lives, seeking opportunities for learning, reflection, and personal development to cultivate a greater sense of purpose, fulfillment, and well-being.

By embracing temperament awareness as a catalyst for personal growth and development, individuals can unlock their full potential, cultivate meaningful relationships, and lead fulfilling lives aligned with their values and aspirations.